KAT MCDIVITT

THE SUCCESS ZONE

A ROADMAP FOR ENTREPRENEURIAL SUCCESS

A B ANGELICO BOOKS

TABLE OF CONTENTS

Introduction

Life begins at the end of your comfort zone.
~ Neale Donald Walsch

It was a rainy Friday in December. I remember leaving work late, and missing dinner again. Eight months into the new business, and already 4 months behind in our business plan. We hadn't yet gotten our first client. I remember looking at the project plan and thinking – "When I worked in Corporate, this would be done by now".

I kept working harder and staying longer because I had a big dream. I wanted to make a difference AND be able to financially support my family and community.

I looked back on what I had produced that week – not much. Another whole week passed and I didn't have much to show for it. It seemed like everything took twice as long as it should – or maybe I spent too much time on things that were just not important. I'm not even sure where I was going wrong.

I felt like I was trying to drive with the handbrake on. We would have some progress, then something would go wrong.

I got home and looked at our little Christmas tree, and the sparse gifts below. We'd had to return the bright new bicycle we'd gotten 12-year old John (my step-son), so the tree looked sparser than ever. He greeted me at the door with a bounce and a smile, and I remember holding back the tears of frustration and sadness.

I rushed through the house and escaped to our 'home office' in the corner of the bedroom. I was confused and angry. I was a project manager. I studied productivity. I wasn't making any progress. I was devoting every iota of energy, passion, time and focus that I had to this business and I was going nowhere!

I felt useless and worthless. Things seemed to work for other people, but not for me. I remember picking up an article my (very successful) friend Pete had printed out for me and asked me to read. I had always been too busy to read it.

That rainy night I sat down and read it. It changed my life. It was about the core differences between how very successful people work vs. how most people work.

When I say 'core', I mean fundamental – starting from the inside out. Once I understood the difference and figured out how to implement it, my life changed.

You see, most people, when they want to be more productive – to get more done – they work from the outside in. They try to change their behaviors or their environment.

I don't know if you've ever had this experience… You want to be more productive, so you try a new productivity technique, or re-start one from the past. It works great for the first few times (or maybe even first few weeks) and then slowly you revert back to the same habits and patterns you've had since school. I know that was my pattern.

What I learned is that really successful people have different habits and patterns. It's not hard for them to stay productive because they've set up their entire lives to be productive. The difference is that they start from the inside out. They don't start with new time management tools. They start by having a clear connection with their passion and working on their beliefs.

You see what they've learned is that it's a lot easier and faster to change your beliefs and have those changes cascade into the rest of your life, to change from the inside out, than to start on the outside with habits and time management systems. One reason is because if there is a conflict between your beliefs and your habits, beliefs almost always win.

One metaphor that can be useful in thinking about this is that of an operating system. Research has shown that in some ways we're like computers (or they are like us), in that we run the same routines over and over in our lives. Basic ones, like how to breathe, and how to get to work, and even how we respond when someone is angry.

These routines are imprinted from our family and community as we are growing up. We'll talk about this more in later chapters.

The key point here though is that when we try to make changes on the behavior or environment level, it's like rearranging icons on a computer desktop. It doesn't make much of an impact on the computer's performance. To make a meaningful impact, we need to go into the operating system, our basic beliefs, and make changes.

This is what really successful people know and do. They know that they need to connect with their passion and manage their beliefs in order to produce at a high level.

Once I really understood this and started to apply it to my life, everything shifted.

In the last five years I've been able to live the life many people only dream about. On the work side I created a publishing company with 27 titles, started an ecommerce business that went from zero to high-six figures in less than three years, and wrote a best-selling book. Personally, I learned how to create amazing relationships. I traveled around the world, learning to kite surf in Sri Lanka and taking my family to Scotland for a week-long boat trip on the Lochs. I feel stronger, better, more vibrant and more excited about life than ever before.

It's been such a huge turnaround that many people have asked me how I did it. So I decided to write it out in this book.

What I'm going to share here has transformed people's lives. It has evolved over a decade of experimentation – trying different ideas and testing them.

I'm only going to give you what has worked for me. I've tried a lot of things to create and build my businesses. Many things worked and many things didn't. There are a few things that are really working well for me right now and that's what I focus on in this book.

My goal here is to give you a blueprint to transform yourself and your life so that you can have the level of success you want. I help people go from feeling overwhelmed to having laser focus, from feeling overworked to having balance in their lives, and from missing deadlines to having business success.

I'm going to ask you to really engage with this material. This book can change your life, if you engage it. So turn off Facebook, set aside some time, read the book, do the exercises and watch the changes.

Have you ever felt unmotivated, like you were not sure exactly what you are doing and why you are doing it?

Do you have a big goal? Something that is calling you to succeed? Something that will demand that you grow and take some risks? This might manifest as a restlessness, a sense that your calling is more than you are doing right now.

Have you ever woken up and not been sure about what tasks to do, and maybe even wondered if the success you want is possible for you?

Well, you are not alone. AND, you've taken action. You've picked up this book and are ready to make some changes to accomplish what is most important to you. Congratulations!

I'd like to start by getting some clarity around your dream.

Imagine that you've achieved exactly what you want, whether this is:

- Freedom to do what you want when you want it
- Creating a legacy
- Having all the wealth you want, just the way you want it
- Being a leader in your community
- Feeling really fulfilled by your life, and truly happy

- Understanding how to create what you really want, when you want it.

Write down your deepest desires. These may be specific, like a certain amount of money (say $100,000 a month) or speaking at a TED talk, or having your business listed on the New York Stock Exchange. Spend a minute to really consider what you most want. Now imagine that you have it, exactly the way you want it.

What's the first thing you are going to do? You might go on vacation, buy some new stuff, maybe move. Then what do you do?

What do you do when you can accomplish whatever you want?

I want you to close your eyes now and spend just one minute thinking about your life AFTER you have exactly achieved what you want. Now I have a question to ask you. *What would you do if you could easily get exactly what you are aiming for?*

Now I want you to consider this question. *Why is your life not like that?*

Most people trade their time for money. They wouldn't do what they do every day for free. They're not doing now what they would do when they have what they really want. My goal is for you to have what is most important for you. I want you to follow your genius, fulfill your potential. That's my goal for you as you are reading this book.

I am going to share a step-by-step Success Blueprint for unblocking your productivity so you can create the life you love – one where you move your agenda forward every day, where you are getting the most important things done, and feeling great about it. Imagine what that might be like – to have the success you visualized above.

Now you have it, whatever that is. You now spend time with your family – travel, raise great kids, and maybe start great charities, or start more businesses. Maybe you'd like to invest in things or create amazing new inventions. Maybe it's just to go fishing or surfing. Whatever it is, this book can give you the roadmap to get there.

In this book, we're going to take a deep look at what might be holding you back. We're going to look at some things that you've probably never considered about psychology, culture, neurology and physiology. These are the real things that hold people back.

I want you to move from feeling frustrated and stuck to having it all.

Many times we might tell ourselves:

NO

Not now

I don't have time

Maybe next year.

The truth is that you will never be younger than you are today. Time is your most valuable resource.

So don't wait.

I want you to have it all. I want you to stop living day-to-day. I want you to leave a legacy. I want you to stop having income anxiety. I want you to be confident of where your income comes from. This is the blueprint. The blueprint to your freedom.

Read the entire book and you'll get the opportunity to:

Ask me some questions directly

Download some very powerful exercises – these exercises alone have changed people's lives.

The promise of the book is this: *Create A Success Blueprint to Double Your Productivity in 90 Days*. The blueprint will help you to:

- Understand the perils of Assigned Authority and why it's easier to work for someone else
- Identify and overcome self-sabotage so you can stay on track every day
- Recognise the cornerstone of business success (your values and vision)

- Learn the secret of how successful people work less and get more done
- Implement Growth Hacking and the Business 3.0 Roadmap

CHAPTER 1

Understand the perils of Assigned Authority and why it's easier to work for someone else

"You may encounter many defeats, but you must not be defeated. In fact, it may be necessary to encounter the defeats, so you can know who you are, what you can rise from, how you can still come out of it." ~ Maya Angelou

I didn't start my career wanting to be an entrepreneur.

After five years of university, where I worked in a cafe in the early mornings, lived in my camper van and showered at the gym and studied all day, what I really wanted when I graduated was a stable life and a nice place to live. The stable life and nice home was what I used to visualize to get me through the day.

Then I finished university and went into banking. I thought I'd be helping people, which I love, but instead I was put into a high-pressure sales environment with crazy (and unreachable) goals and lots of competition.

I didn't know that the goals were crazy and unreachable. So I worked really, really hard. I stayed at the bank way past closing time, and used every ounce of creativity to meet my quota of new mortgages and credit cards. On top of this, the bank was a toxic work environment. I remember sitting in the lunchroom on my first day of work and my mentor leaned over and said "I hate Wells Fargo".

I was young, and I trusted the organization to take care of me. That's what I had been taught by my friends, parents, and school.

I believed that the goals set by the bank were reasonable. They made sense when all the Business Banking Officers first learned them. Then they just got bigger. I started missing my targets. I felt that I just wasn't working hard enough when I didn't reach them. I was trained as a little girl that the authority knew best, and if I wasn't stacking up, it must be my fault.

I did reach them. I actually ended up being a top salesperson in Northern California. I got written up, I made a lot of money, and I felt really good about myself. I also stayed late every night, I worked on weekends, and I sold credit cards, mortgages and bank loans like crazy.

Then I burned out and got a chronic immune disease.

I spent two years lying on a couch, barely able to move. I had about 5% of the energy that I had when I was a collegiate athlete, full-time student and part-time cook in college. In those days, my highest achievement in a day was to walk down to the lawn and lie on it for 15 minutes. I was 21, and the doctors told me that this would be my life for the next 60 years – if I was lucky.

I lived that way for two years. *I remember the moment everything changed.*

I was deeply in love, and very tired all the time. One day I walked into a party and saw Christy, a classmate of my boyfriend's looking up at him with that glowy, vibrant 'interested' look in her eyes. Something deep inside of me said, "NO – this is not my life! I'm not willing to lose my career, my health and my relationship."

I made the decision that I was not going to accept this as my life.

That I would do whatever it took to get better. In that moment I decided not to listen to the system, and really started thinking for myself and taking action.

This is how I learned my first lesson – the lesson of Assigned Authority.

No one really talks about Assigned Authority, and I think it is the ugly underpinning of our culture and education – and the number 1 reason entrepreneurs fail.

We're Trained from Birth to Give Away Our Authority

When we're born, we have some sense of identity and innate ability to do things, an *internal authority* of our desires and understanding. And, from the time we're born, almost every time we attempt to assert that authority, we are suppressed.

We are trained as babies to eat on someone else's schedule, sleep on someone else's schedule. The only time we really get to assert our authority is when we poop. And when we're potty trained even that is removed from us.

Then we go to school, and we do what someone else wants us to do on their timetable and they decide if we've done it correctly. Our own internal sense of autonomy, of internal authority is replaced by external authority – the authority of our parents and community.

Using the "Operating System" metaphor, when we are kids, our brains are loaded with the 'operating system' of our community. This is a critical part of staying alive. We needed to learn the rules of our family and community quickly, and follow them without thinking. On some level this is what it means to be a part of a society.

So, this operating system, just like the one on a computer, is designed to run in the background and process everything that comes our way.

It helps us to fit in, to keep us safe, and to work within the system we are born into.

Our preferences, our habits, our beliefs, our ways of approaching problems – these are all set in place at an early age and, until we start to become conscious of them, they are largely automatic. They are part of the operating system.

For most of us this means that we listen to those in authority. We follow, we don't lead. We give our power to an *External Authority:* our parents, our teachers and our employers.

When I was a child I lived near the largest radio telescope in the world (at that time). The two things that were really cool about that were the swimming pool, and being able to play Adventure on the super-computer (don't tell Cornell University). We would go into the huge server room with millions of dollars of equipment and sit at the very modern (for the times) computers and geek out.

Now I have more computing power on my iPhone than there was in that multi-million dollar server room.

In the same way, the brain, and skills and abilities that you had as a 7-year old, when most of your beliefs were being finalized, is very much less powerful than the brain that you have today. But, unlike Cornell University (who I guess has probably upgraded their systems), most people are still running the old programs on their adult mind that they were running as a child.

Those old programs run in the background and therefore many parts of our lives run on autopilot and we don't think too hard about why we do some of the things we do.

When you become an entrepreneur, autopilot isn't enough. You are creating something out of nothing, learning new skills and enlisting support for your vision from your community. You want to fulfill your potential in a new way. And you don't do that by doing the same old things in the same old way. You need to upgrade your operating system. Let's talk about where your original operating system comes from – society and often our educational system.

Just as you are running an old operating system in your mind, our global culture is running Education 1.0 in a world that really needs Education 2.0. More than that, entrepreneurs need to be running Education 3.0. Time for an upgrade!

What is school for?

The old education system (Education 1.0) was designed to standardise knowledge and mold young minds into conformity, destined for the factory floor. Sitting in rows in front of a teacher who teaches you the 'truth'. Our educational system was created in the age of the Industrial Revolution in order to:

- Create a society that is culturally coordinated
- Train people to be productive (factory) workers
- Build an economy of compliant workers and eager consumers

In other words, to create "compliant, competitive zombies" as Seth Godin would put it (see reference below).

The father of our education system, Horace Mann, wrote:

Building a person's character was just as important as reading, writing and arithmetic. By instilling values such as obedience to authority, promptness in attendance, and organizing the time according to bell ringing helped students prepare for future employment.

The method to create this was to amplify fear and suppress or destroy passion.

The system doesn't promote the kind of thinking that makes good entrepreneurs and leaders. It doesn't encourage us to dream outside of what we already know – to think outside the box. Seth Godin, in his manifesto on education *Stop Stealing Dreams* says:

> *"I think we're doing a great job of destroying dreams at the very same time the dreams we do hold onto aren't nearly bold enough."*

If you missed out on the upgrade when you were at school, it's not too late to learn how to dream big dreams, and make them into reality. The things we are talking about in this book can change all that. We're not talking about a patch here. Together, we can take your glitchy old operating system and give it a complete overhaul.

Here's what I mean:

As we grow up, when we try to assert our own internal authority or creativity, it's often squashed. We're trained to become followers of some external authority (parents, teachers, societal norms), not leaders listening to our own internal authority.

As a side note, it's interesting that many successful entrepreneurs were rebels to the 'system' when they were young. There's a good reason for that.

A new research paper from the National Bureau for Economic Research (http://www.nber.org/papers/w19276) reports that entrepreneurs often:

- Are intelligent
- Have high self-esteem
- Had a higher level of risky and even illicit behavior as adolescents

Bill Gates was arrested as a teenager. Richard Branson dropped out of high school at 15. Winston Churchill failed the sixth grade. Charles Darwin also failed to impress at school and was considered by "all my masters and my father, a very ordinary boy, rather below the common standard of intellect".

Thinking in the Workplace

When we get a job (like my job at the bank), we are again told that, to succeed, we must follow the External Authorities rules. If we don't follow the rules, we can be reprimanded or even fired. Our job is to fit in, do what they want when and how they want us to to do it. I remember being told over and over in my life: "Don't question authority".

The external structure of school and society is like an exoskeleton that is created around us to keep us productive in the world around us. At the same time, our internal authority is atrophying.

Most people don't see it. It's so much a part of our lives and how we live that we can't observe it. We swim in the sea of our culture – hanging out with the other fish, gathering around the fish water cooler.

Then we decide to leave the ocean and venture onto land, and we lose all that support.

When We Become Entrepreneurs We Lose Our Support Structure of Success

At some point though, either through inspiration or through desperation, we say "f$#& it, I'm going to go start my own company". And the exoskeleton – the system supporting our productivity transforms from a supporting structure, to a cage or suit of armor that doesn't allow us to be as free and agile as we now need to be.

That's when entrepreneurs become massively unproductive, especially solopreneurs. Without that external support system, most entrepreneurs fail and end up on the beach, gasping for air, wondering why they feel so unproductive.

What I have seen working as a project coach over the last 10 years is that entrepreneurs in this state get 1/4 to 1/8 done of what they think they could get done. They are easily distracted, they don't have a clear plan of action, they don't work on the hard stuff. Then they beat themselves up. They put themselves down. And they try an external time management technique which doesn't work. They don't understand what is really going on.

It's Not Your Fault

What most people don't realize is that it's not an internal failing. It's not a lack of willpower or intelligence, or motivation. Actually, we've been trained by our culture to be unproductive on our own.

How Do We Grow Our Internal Authority?

The solution is to build up our internal authority – to adopt the beliefs and habits that differentiate the highly successful entrepreneurs from the others.

To grow legs and learn to succeed in a whole different world.

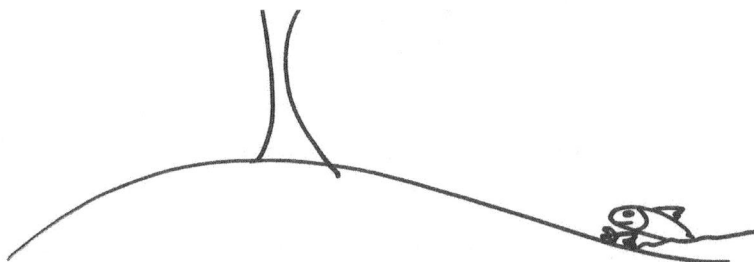

Most entrepreneurs face one or more of the following challenges:

1.   They have an Employee Operating System rather than an Entrepreneur Operating System

The dominant paradigm for most people is working for someone else. Most people grew up with parents who worked for someone else, or went through schools where they were taught about work and following someone else's schedule. That's what their parents did, that's what the people around them do, that is how they've been trained. When they go off on their own they struggle to have a clear vision of their own, to find the internal discipline and confidence to create their own systems to get things done, and to influence people around them to come on board with their vision.

2.   Motivation – Finding and connecting with your values as the source of ongoing motivation and passion – even when things are really difficult.

3.   Success Roadmap – Creating and following a clear path to get from where you are to the success you want to attain.

These are the topics that we'll be covering in detail in the rest of this book.

Summary

After the banking debacle and getting sick I tried everything – from quack remedies to expensive medical specialists in San Francisco. Eventually I started to have more energy, less brain fog, and I was able to go back to work. Over time I made it up to about 80%, which I'm grateful for every day. I still need to manage my energy and my health, and I've developed healthy habits to keep me feeling good.

So, what did I learn from working at the bank? It was a difficult time and process, and what I learned that has really helped me is to:

- Listen to my own inner voice – to trust my intuition and not follow 'authority' blindly.
- That it's dangerous and unhealthy to turn my authority over to someone else. I need to be the keeper of my authority. It doesn't mean I can't listen to other people and work with them. Ultimately, though, my goals are to care for me, and their goals are to care for themselves (or their organization).
- I learned to build my own internal authority, and that's what we'll be talking about through the rest of the book.

This crude map shows that belief without motivation produces no action, that motivation without belief produces self sabotage, and that success requires all three components: belief, motivation, and a roadmap.

Here's a quick overview of how we'll be talking about it in this book:

Chapter 2: You can have the motivation to succeed, and a clear roadmap of success but, if you don't believe you can succeed you might sabotage your own success. Many people do.

Chapter 3: You can have the beliefs and the roadmap of how to succeed, but if you are not motivated to do the work, then it won't happen.

Chapter 4: You can have the beliefs and the motivation, but if you don't know what to do, you won't get there in the quickest way possible.

Putting it all together. When you have the beliefs that you can succeed, the motivation to do the work, and the roadmap of exactly what to do, then success comes more easily.

CHAPTER 2

The Success Comfort Zone: How We Unconsciously Sabotage Our Success

"Many of life's failures are people who did not realize how close they were to success when they gave up."
~ Thomas A. Edison

Peter looked out over Seattle and wondered what had happened. In the last six weeks his life had completely imploded. His business had failed spectacularly, leaving him with crippling debt, his wife walked out, and his daily relationship with red wine started to be the most fulfillment he had in his life.

The 'official diagnosis' was a nervous breakdown. It felt like he couldn't do anything. Nothing. He had pushed himself to the wall and then hit a series of roadblocks. He wondered: "How did I go from being an executive at the largest advertising agency in the state and being involved in an exciting high-tech start-up to sitting at the bar every night?"

It seemed like everything was going so well! He had customers, he was making money, he was feeling great, and then one thing after another fell apart. He had a suspicion that he was the cause of the problems, and he didn't know how and what to change. After awhile his new life as a business failure settled into a routine. Sleep all day, start to look at job advertisements in the afternoon, then go to the bar. Eventually his friend Sarah convinced him to reach out to me and we started working together.

This story is not unusual – maybe a few differences. Men tend to end up drinking or doing drugs, women tend to end up depressed and sleeping all the time. The similarity is that they start to see a pattern of destruction in their lives, and realize that it's not bad luck. It's them.

One big reason entrepreneurs fail is because we are taught to limit ourselves as children. The operating system we were given as children had clear parameters around the concept of "success". When we make some headway in breaking out of the mold of our childhood – when we start to have some success – our system revolts (our hard drive crashes). It's like we have a 'Success Comfort Zone', and when we leave that zone our system does everything it can to bring us back to that place where we are comfortable.

For example, I learned in my childhood that being seen and standing out was dangerous. My sisters and I were taught to always be gracious, and to never make waves. If we did make waves, we were punished by the Authorities (our parents). By the time I was in high school I did everything I could to not be the center of attention because being seen was not safe in my mind.

Then, when my business started to take off, when I started being seen as an expert, when all the really important people in town knew my name, I got petrified and sabotaged my own success.

When I started doing accountability coaching, I realized that it was wasn't just me.

Earlier this month I was talking to a client who does really well when he starts a project. He zooms ahead and gets lots done and has a lot of early success, then things start to go wrong.

He loses momentum, and his project slowly grinds to a halt. He feels stuck. He gets almost to launch time and then it feels like he's walking through quicksand, getting more and more bogged down.

This happens over and over for him – this same pattern is in his current business, and in the last business.

What is really frustrating to him is that he knows exactly what to do – he has a clear plan – he's just not doing it. He knew something had to change or his business would get sucked under and he would lose everything. He just couldn't work out what needed to change.

That's what happened to me, I felt like if I really went out into the world and marketed our products and made a big splash, I would be unsafe. Deep in my unconscious mind I had decided that I would rather be safe than be successful. Until I could shift that belief I really couldn't be either safe OR successful.

The Biggest Reason Entrepreneurs Fail

Have you ever felt frustrated because you're not making the progress that you know you are capable of and it feels like something is holding you back? Do you ever suspect that you are holding yourself back, and you don't see how?

If so, you are not alone. I hear this story or something similar almost every day. And I understand because I used to do the exact same thing. I was lucky though – I learned what is really going on, and was able to shift it.

You see, what I've learned in the last 10 years is that it's generally a mindset issue. One thing that really holds entrepreneurs back is that 'old operating system'. The set of beliefs that supports us in being 'followers', in being workers in our cultural system. But doesn't support us in being successful entrepreneurs. If you have these issues, life can be very difficult until you can update this programming.

That's why all the great business success coaches from Dale Carnegie and Napoleon Hill to the biggest business leaders of today like Oprah Winfrey, Richard Branson and Warren Buffett talk about what and how you think. Many of their core success factors are not about how to build a business, they are about how to think about your business, how to manage your mindset, and how to keep going when things get tough.

Your business will ultimately live or die based on your mindset, beliefs, and the habits that you have based on those beliefs. And all of that comes back to your identity and values. Do you think of yourself as a successful entrepreneur? If not, why not? That key shift in your identity will have a cascading effect on everything you do.

One interesting exercise is to think about a really successful entrepreneur – one you really admire. For me it would be Richard Branson. Then, as you move through your day, ask yourself: what would a successful entrepreneur (Richard Branson) do in this situation? How would he/she think about this setback or challenge?

Really successful entrepreneurs take care of their health, they have a supportive morning routine, they have good teams around them, and they have a strong connection with their values and vision. That vision informs everything they do in their business, and often in their life. They understand that setbacks are just another source of information (not a reflection on themselves), and they are comfortable with the idea of success.

Changing beliefs is easier than changing behaviors

What you might not realize is that your patterns and beliefs around your success, what you are capable of and what you are 'allowed' to achieve were created as a young child. This is your Success Comfort Zone. The space where you are comfortable being successful.

These patterns and beliefs of our old operating system are kind of sneaky because most people don't see them – we see through them (like a set of lenses) – and we are subject to them until we can look at them directly and update them into beliefs that support our success. This is the number one reason entrepreneurs fail.

This is the first area where super-successful people are different from everyone else.

Here's how it works.

You have a belief that you developed in childhood, probably from your family (there are five core beliefs that cause most of the issues, and I'll talk about those later in this chapter).

Then you have some level of success higher than your comfort zone – maybe in your business, or in your family, or even in your level of happiness.

This success is in conflict with the belief about 'how life should be' that you developed in your childhood. It creates a conflict in your brain. The technical term is 'cognitive dissonance'.

What that means is that your system/brain has the conflicting experiences of success in your life or business and the belief of 'how life should be'. It can resolve this conflict in one of two ways:

1. Let go of 'how life should be' – which is possible only if you are aware that you have the conflict
2. Get rid of the success, usually through self-sabotage

Your brain, in order to relieve the stress and bring your reality back into your Success Comfort Zone, usually finds a creative way to sabotage your success and neutralize the stress. Often this is through self-sabotage.

This could easily have been my story 10 years ago. I felt perpetually stuck. Actually I felt stuck for years, in lots of areas of my life, money, success, my health and my relationships. I was all around stuck.

I've spent the last 10 years studying this issue, learning about neuroscience, mindset, physiology and psychology. I've spent thousands of dollars on training and hundreds of hours working one-on-one with people helping them with limiting beliefs and self-sabotage.

This idea has been identified and studied by lots of people. For example, Gay Hendricks (author of Conscious Loving) in The Big Leap identifies four major self-sabotaging beliefs. In the work that I do with people I consider an additional category of beliefs, bringing it to five limiting beliefs. These beliefs are part of our core operating system. At one point they helped us survive and fit in with our community expectations. But, we may need to update them.

So, what exactly is a belief?

What is a belief? A belief is what you believe to be true. It is something you feel certain about. But that doesn't mean that your belief is true, or that it is true for someone else, or that you necessarily have a verified foundation for this certainty. Beliefs change over time.

For example, in the 14th century everyone (who was anyone) believed that the sun went around the earth. This was the common wisdom and supported by the research of the day. In fact, when Galileo shared his research that showed that the earth in fact circles the sun, he was branded as a heretic and put under house arrest. That shows how very much society clings to our beliefs. People were completely unwilling to even consider that the Earth was not the center of the universe. Now we know that in fact, the earth circles the sun and this fundamental belief about the world has changed.

In the same way many people have beliefs about themselves For example: "I could never be good at public speaking", or "I'm not smart enough to finish university". Then they take some classes and have some successes and their beliefs change.

It's important to keep in mind that our beliefs are not us, and we are not our beliefs. A belief is something we have. It is something we can cultivate and change to give us more in our lives. A belief is not immutable.

But because we believe that our beliefs are immutable, we allow them to shape our reality.

For a quick example, think of something you are good at now. Let's say you are a good at walking, or racket ball, or using a computer. At some point, you probably were not good at it, and you might have had the belief "I'm not good at this" which would be true because, in fact, you were not. Now though, you are. So you have transformed this belief.

I worked with a woman who was second in command of a small start-up. She always thought of herself as a project manager. That was her belief. She was a project manager and she had a role in the company as a project manager.

The company was going well and, because she was a good decision maker, she was encouraged to step up into the leadership team. But once she was in the leadership team, her decision-making started getting worse.

With support from her mentor, she had been the backbone of the success of the company, but without that support she started making bad decisions and becoming insecure.

When I first started working with her she didn't see it as a belief issue. She thought to herself "I'm not good enough, and I'm from India, and so I can never be a manager". She took on that belief as true and it impacted her work. She was hitting her own level of discomfort. She wanted to be a manager, and she had a fear of breaking out of the mold that she had cast herself in.

Working together for one month we were able to work through the beliefs that were keeping her from having the same quality of work at the management level that she had at the operations level. Once she was able to let go of that deeply held belief about her management potential, she was able to accelerate her promotion within the company.

Here's a list of beliefs that can slow us down:

1. It's best to work many hours every day
2. I need to do it all myself
3. I should be able to do this faster
4. It's my fault that X

5. I need more research to take action
6. It needs to be perfect before I can put it into the world
7. There isn't enough
8. Being successful is hard
9. Failure is a bad thing

What I've discovered is that most limiting beliefs fall into five general groupings. Let's explore each one.

The 5 primary beliefs that destroy your productivity

As you read about them, stop with each one and see how it feels for you. If it sounds even a little true for you, then there's real value in checking it out. Some people find that none of these beliefs ring true for them, often this is because there is a layer of beliefs over the core belief that is hiding the core belief.

1. I'm broken, worthless or not good enough. If some part of you (that little kid part) feels like you are broken or worthless and then you have amazing success, that sets up an internal conflict that your system will generally resolve through self-sabotage.
2. If I'm too big or bright, I'll be knocked down. This is the fear that if we're big, we'll paint a target on ourselves and be attacked. It's not safe to be successful.
3. If I'm too successful, I'll be disloyal to my family. This is often about our role in our original biological family. Breaking out of our role is often seen as shameful and disloyal and can reflect on the entire family. We're afraid that our success will cause us to be ostracized.
4. If I'm too successful, I'll be a burden to those around me. We want to fit in and be liked, and sometimes if we're too successful it makes the people around us uncomfortable.

5. If I break out of my cultural stereotype I'll be shunned. It goes something like this "X people are not successful." Where X is 'old', 'young', 'educational level', 'skin tone', 'culture'. It's the belief that people 'like you' can not be successful.

When you hold these beliefs and you start to succeed and get everything you want, it creates a conflict in your system. Your external reality and your internal map of beliefs no longer match up and that can feel uncomfortable as our subconscious tries to redress the balance. If we don't do something specific about it, the way our system deals with this internal conflict is self-sabotage.

Self-sabotage comes in lots of different flavors, including:

*   getting sick
*   getting distracted and spending time on Facebook
*   losing focus
*   'bright shiny objects' – always chasing the next new thing
*   getting into a fight with our partner

The solution is to get to the heart of the matter – to resolve the internal conflict around your success, then find the limiting belief and transform it to a new supportive belief. I'm going to give some very specific actions you can take to resolve that internal conflict at the end of the chapter.

Fear of Change

What gets in the way of making these changes?

Fear of change trumps fear of failure every time. For a lot of people, change has a deeply unconscious linkage with death. I'm guessing fear of dying isn't something that you think about every day – at least consciously. You might be surprised about how your unconscious mind can equate success and death.

The theory is that as a biological being, living in tribes, new things were dangerous. If we found a new plant or a new animal or a new place, we didn't know the dangers that lurked within them. Our deep unconscious programming is to be very cautious of the new.

In the modern world, while your life now may be difficult and frustrating, one thing that your system knows is that you can handle it. It is familiar. Your body and soul know that you can survive everything that you have in your life right now because you are already doing it.

Look around – you are currently alive.

When you look at that thing 'out there' – that success that you want so badly – well, that is unfamiliar. You haven't been there yet. That's why it's scary.

Your system doesn't know that you will survive it. Your basic purpose in life is to continue to exist. As long as you continue to exist there is hope.

When you go out and try something new – when you reach for new heights – if you are like most people there is a big chunk of your brain that doesn't want you to reach that goal because it is new and unfamiliar. That part of your brain is not sure that you'll survive if you reach that goal. You are leaving your Success Comfort Zone. So it sabotages your success.

Entrepreneurs can struggle more than most with the fear of change. They are operating outside of corporate structures where there are whole teams of change management, legal and human resource professionals making it safe for the business to move forward.

When you add limiting beliefs to the fear of change it can really stop your business from moving forward at all. This is why often entrepreneurs will do really well for a while, then progress will just stop.

As an entrepreneur you need to tackle your fears alone, for the most part. That's why the most successful people in business are continuously investing in their own personal development, by utilizing coaches and mentors, who can help them to work through their fears and explore or integrate them into a plan of action.

Without professional support, you can thrash away at your fears and make incremental steps towards your goal. That's ok, but it can take a lot of time – time you could be spending enjoying your success.

Many entrepreneurs hit the upper limit of their success zone and get knocked down and don't really understand what's going on. They think it's external and they cast themselves as a victim. Then they pick themselves up and go for it again.

They are like Don Quixote, tilting at windmills. They pick themselves up, and maybe this time their success zone moves up a fraction. Each time, they make a bit more progress, but it's painful – they might make some progress, but then something happens to prove them wrong: they have a nervous breakdown, they cannot sustain their relationship, or they struggle with their health. As long as they view the problem as external to themselves, it will be more difficult to achieve the success they desire.

There are three ways to solve this situation (all of which I've tried and they have helped me move my business forward).

1. *Beating against it.* If you keep thrashing against your comfort zone, you'll either expand, or you'll be completely exhausted. This is the most stressful and least effective solution. When you feel that internal conflict (and you'll notice it now that you know that it exists), you consciously choose to let go of the belief that you "can't" rather than self-sabotaging. My experience with this technique is that when I use it I tend to feel strong emotions around the issue – fear, frustration, isolation – and I go ahead and do it anyway. It does work (slowly), however I'd rather put my time and energy into my business being successful. So I looked for other options.

2. *Psychotherapy.* Years of therapy can help identify and unravel unhelpful patterns and beliefs, if you find the right therapist and want to focus on that approach. Again, while therapy has helped me a lot, I'd rather focus on my business rather than spending years of my life and hundreds of thousands of dollars in therapy.

3. *The Success Zone Program.* I studied limiting beliefs for 10 years testing and determining what works, and what doesn't. Based on all of this research and experimentation I created a program called the Success Zone which helps people identify and transform limiting beliefs. One very powerful belief change exercise is below:

   a. Take out a sheet of paper (or open a new document on your computer) and write down 5 thoughts, actions or habits you currently have that you think keep you from being successful.

   b. Write down what kinds of beliefs someone might need in order to have these thoughts, actions or habits.

   c. Now look at the basic categories of limiting beliefs:

      • Not good enough/ broken
      • If I get big I'll be a target/unsafe
      • Changing will be disloyal
      • Being successful will mean I'm a burden
      • I'm too X {tall, short, dark, light, young, old...} to be successful

   d. Notice if any of these beliefs look/feel/sound familiar.

   e. Now look at the proof – on both sides. What supports this claim? What refutes it? Do you have evidence on both sides?

   f. Consider if this belief has value in your life, either now or when you were a child. Many beliefs start when we are children, and their purpose is to keep us safe. They might not be doing a great job of it now, though, but that's what they are trying to accomplish.

g. Now choose a belief you would like to have instead.

h. Start looking for evidence of this new belief every day.

This is one simple exercise for changing limiting beliefs. If this one doesn't work for you right away, then don't stop. Try another one! We have several belief change exercises on the Success Zone Book page. (http://angelicobooks.com/success)

I wish I had had these techniques when I discovered my limiting beliefs! Unfortunately I didn't, and for me, sorting out my limiting beliefs was not a quick fix.

I did eventually find my way out of the darkness. Over the next ten years I did deep research into the latest thinking in productivity, psychology, and neural research. I tried a lot of things, and started to see what really worked, and what was just hype and wishful thinking.

So the first step in creating an Internal Authority locus of control – as opposed to an External Authority – is to start to look at your beliefs, and shift them.

CHAPTER 3

Access Your Power: The Keystone to Business Success

"The difference between a successful person and others is not a lack of strength, not a lack of knowledge, but rather a lack in will." ~ Vince Lombardi, Jr.

My next business I did things differently. By that time I understood the issue of Assigned Authority and my own limiting beliefs. I realized that I needed a coach in order to help me stay focused and get things done.

On one hand I felt like I couldn't afford a coach, especially as a struggling entrepreneur. The only coach I interviewed who seemed like they could really help hold me accountable charged over $2,000 a month, which was about half of what I was earning.

On the other hand, I also knew I couldn't afford not to have a coach. So I bit the bullet and did it. It was one of the best decisions I've ever made. Having the structure of an external authority (my coach) helped me to get organized and made me at least 200% more productive. I went from getting about one hour of solid work done every day, to being really amazingly focused and productive, and my income increased 4X as well.

As I mentioned earlier, I had trouble staying on track. I realized that all my life I'd worked for money, and I never had to come up with my own business idea. Even the business I was working in at the time (a web technology business) wasn't my own idea. I was in the grocery store one day and a friend came up to me and asked me to create a website for him. I told him I didn't know anything about web design, and he asked me if I could figure it out. I had moved through my issues around taking risks and I figured out how to create a simple website. Three years later I had a team of designers and programmers and was living in Hawaii a block from Kailua beach, one of the most beautiful beaches in the world.

Still, my limiting beliefs kept cropping up, so I wanted some external authority – someone to help me to blast through the barriers that my limiting beliefs were putting up. I got a productivity coach to help me figure out what I needed, and to hold me accountable. He provided all the authority I needed to be successful. He had a very well-defined coaching modality, and I was willing to give him some authority.

This arrangement worked great for the first two years. My business grew and I felt like I had everything completely under control.

Then I started chafing at the control. In my coach's world there was 'one right way'. He was all about command and control – scheduling out every moment and using external devices to manage my life. I remember walking along Kailua beach one day thinking that, while my life was completely organized, I was miserable. His mold of how to be productive didn't work for me anymore.

I also realized that I was only running that business to make money. I had jumped from the frying pan into the fire. I had re-created a 'job', and instead of working for someone else and being able to go home at

5 p.m. every day, I was working late into the night, every night. I wasn't inspired by the work. I wasn't motivated or passionate. There were many days where I just went through the motions, and it showed.

I finally realized that I had no motivation for my new 'work', and for me to be super successful and have fun, I was going to need to find my own motivation – to be excited about my work every day. I wasn't passionate.

One of my side jobs at the time was mentoring companies who were seeking Venture Capital, and they were always very passionate about their businesses. I got very curious about the difference between them and me.

So I went on another quest to understand what keeps entrepreneurs motivated. What keeps us motivated? What keeps us going when things get rough?

In the corporate world, our initial motivation may be money. We need to make a certain amount of money to live a comfortable life. Then, once basic needs are met, research cited by productivity and business author Daniel Pink indicates that the secondary motivations are:

- *Autonomy* – something that entrepreneurs want a ton of!
- *Mastery* – something we often have less of
- *Purpose* – connecting to a greater cause gives us a high level of motivation

In our 'jobs' our managers set the goals, set the pace, and created the higher purpose and motivation. And many of us (including me) just accepted them as our own.

Then, when we go out on our own, that motivation ebbs and flows. It's often easy to lose motivation because:

- We're tired
- We don't know exactly how to do a certain task
- We don't have someone to bounce ideas off of

- Everything means a whole lot more – it's our business!

Research (*Entrepreneurial Resilience: Real & Perceived Barriers to Implementing Entrepreneurial Intentions – Norris F. Krueger, Jr., Ph.D.*) indicates that resilience is one of the key factors to entrepreneurial success.

One of the key elements of resilience and of motivation is having a clear connection between your values and your vision.

The way you learn is to deeply access your own inner values and be able to clearly articulate that in an engaging vision to your team and your customers.

We need to learn how to connect our values and create a vision. Ideally one as powerful as John F. Kennedy did with his generation-defining vision of putting a man on the moon.

What is Vision and Why Do We Need It?

On May 25, 1961, President John F. Kennedy announced before a special joint session of Congress the dramatic and ambitious goal of sending an American safely to the Moon before the end of the decade. At the time of Kennedy's proposal, only one American had flown in space, and NASA had never even sent an astronaut into orbit.

It was a huge goal, and the technology to achieve it had not even been envisioned yet. No one actually knew how to do it, or if it could even be done. Landing astronauts on the Moon by the end of 1969 required a burst of technological creativity and the largest commitment of resources ($24 billion) that had ever been made by a nation in peacetime.

On July 20, 1969, astronauts Neil Armstrong and Buzz Aldrin became the first humans to ever set foot on a world beyond planet Earth.

The moon landing was a huge achievement for humanity and a huge boost to American technological pride.

This vision of doing the impossible task motivated an entire decade of people. It was a huge vision, and from that huge vision came thousands of people's jobs and billions of dollars in spending. In order to accomplish the vision in the short timeframe, the vision needed to be crystal clear and motivate people to take action.

The vision motivated and mobilized the country because it was framed to leverage our key values and our key fears at the time – security and self-worth. We, as a country, were feeling threatened by the soviet advances and a vision that promised a new era of achievement targeted these underlying values and leveraged them to create a huge vision that shaped our country.

NASA already had a plan to get to the moon in measured, incremental steps. They might even have made it to the moon some day. What Kennedy did was shake up the timeline. Given how difficult and expensive space travel is, if Kennedy had not had the vision and made it public and brought the entire country (and a significant budget) behind it, we might still be looking up at the moon and wondering if it was made of green cheese.

Just like Kennedy, super-successful entrepreneurs are able to understand their own values and their client values, create a compelling vision and use it to keep themselves and their stakeholders motivated.

Vision is the manifestation of your values into action

JFK's vision was "Put a man on the moon". Simple, clear, focused, and it drove an entire decade of innovation and national pride and millions of dollars of funding.

Your vision is where you are going – your big goal, or dream. It is what you most want to accomplish.

Your vision – is rooted in your values. Values are what spark our passions, keep us motivated, and what help us make choices.

If you look at the underlying values of the Apollo Mission, the key value that motivated the nation was security. There were certainly other benefits in terms of the advancement of technology, economic benefits, benefits in national morale and such, but the underlying value where JFK connected with the American people to make this happen was the benefit of national safety and security.

When the connection between values and vision is strong, things tend to work well. It's when they break down that people lose focus and things become ill-defined and, frankly, uncomfortable.

Refer to the diagram on the next page to show what I'm getting at:

If you want to take your business or your team to the next level, you need to get clear on your vision (and I'll give you an exercise on how to do this at the end of the chapter). Being clear on your vision has a myriad of benefits:

1. It helps you to stay motivated every day.
2. It makes creating a Success Roadmap (which we'll discuss in the next chapter) much easier.
3. It helps you understand your Highest Lifetime Goals. There is a thread between your choices and your highest lifetime values. That thread is what gives you motivation to do what needs to be done in your business.

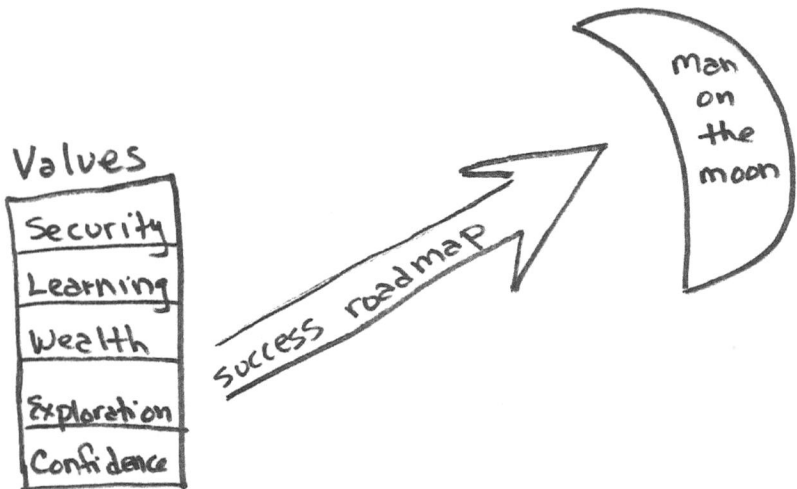

Values and Motivation

Your energy and focus – your motivation – comes from being connected to your highest values and expressing them through your vision and your Success Roadmap. This is what will give you the flexibility and resilience to bounce back and change course when you need to.

So let's take this step by step and understand:

1. What values are and why are they important
2. What your vision is and what is the difference between having a set vision and one inspired by values
3. How having a clear sense of direction helps you make decisions on your Highest Value Activities.

What are values?

Values are what are most important to you. They are the things you deeply believe are important in the way you live and work. They are different for everyone. They ultimately determine your priorities and how you measure if you are going in the right direction in your life, or if you've been blown off course.

Here are some values that many entrepreneurs resonate with:

- Freedom
- Security
- Contribution
- Fulfillment
- Creativity
- Autonomy

Your values are a part of your 'why'.

When you start from your vision – your 'why' – the 'what' and the 'how' of what you do in your business, and in your life, will follow with ease. Being clear about your vision also helps to enlist people into your business, your team… your vision. When you are clear about your vision, you make it easy for people to follow you. Simon Sinak, in his book *Start with Why: How Great Leaders Inspire Everyone to Take Action*, says 'People don't buy what you do, they buy why you do it'. People buy the proof of your beliefs – the end product of your vision.

When your actions align with your values, then life tends to go smoothly. You have alignment in your system and you don't have so many internal conflicts (we'll talk about this later). When your actions, goals and vision do not line up with your values, things feel more difficult and stressful. This misalignment can lead to a lack of focus – it's hard to get things done, and in the long run it can lead to dissatisfaction and depression.

Your values can change over your lifetime, and can be fulfilled by short or long-term goals. You can have values around your business, and values around your personal life.

Generally, people define what is really important to them in their lives in one or more of these 5 areas:

- *Acquiring* – the new car, the house, the things
- *Accomplishment and recognition* – I want to do this and be seen and heard for it
- *Belonging* – being part of a community or a group
- *Experiencing*
- *Learning*

Some common expressions of values include:

Achievement:	reaching goals through prowess and proficiency
Activity:	an appreciation of physical or mental undertakings and fast-moving action

Advancement:	progress, development and superiority as a result of hard work
Adventure:	new experiences, exciting feats, new ventures
Aesthetics:	an appreciation of beauty
Affiliation:	alignment or association with certain people, organizations or groups
Affluence:	prosperity, financial and material abundance
Authority:	planning, commanding and deciding, being in charge
Autonomy:	self-reliance, independence from outside influence
Balance:	achieving a state of equilibrium in different areas of life
Challenge:	testing skills and abilities in the pursuit of knowledge, physical superiority or gain
Change and variation:	diversity in environment, people and ideas
Collaboration:	working productively with people or teams
Community:	being part of a group of people who have a common purpose or interests
Compassion:	empathy and thoughtfulness towards others
Competence:	demonstrating efficiency in skills and knowledge
Competition:	pitting your skills against others
Contribution:	making a difference

Courage:	resilience and confidence in the presence of danger, fear or suffering
Creativity:	using imagination and resourcefulness to innovate
Diverse perspectives:	appreciation of varied points of view that are out of the ordinary
Duty:	responsibility, obligation
Economic security:	stable cash flow that assures your chosen standard of living
Enjoyment:	pleasure, joy and amusement
Fame:	recognition, stature or reputation from your achievements
Family:	the importance of links to people in your extended family group
Freedom:	being free of restrictions of movement, expression, association and thought
Friendship:	developing close bonds with other people
Happiness:	satisfaction and joy
Health:	physiological well-being and vitality
Helping others:	assisting others to reach their potential
Humor:	joy, appreciating the funny side of life
Influence:	motivating others to action
Integrity:	principled, moral, ethical
Justice:	impartiality, a clear sense of right and wrong
Knowledge:	mastery through learning

Location:	geographical location is important to you
Love:	tenderness, affection, acceptance, commitment, fondness and attachment towards and from other people
Loyalty:	allegiance and devotion to people, organizations or ideas
Order:	stability, predictability, established procedures
Personal development:	improving abilities, psychological, physical and emotional state to achieve your utmost potential in life
Physical fitness:	overall state of health, strength, vitality
Recognition:	acknowledgement and appreciation for your achievements
Reflection:	contemplation, thoughtful consideration
Responsibility:	obligation towards a person, organization or society
Safety:	feeling protected
Self-respect:	self esteem, dignity, self-worth
Spirituality:	connection to something greater than ourselves
Status:	position or standing in relation to society, authority or rank
Security:	being free from danger
Wisdom:	discernment, deep reflection on information, experiences and skills

Values & Motivation & Passion

So why do we care so much about values? How does this relate to productivity?

Our values help us access our passion and our motivation.

Passion is the fire that burns and energizes you to get through a rough meeting, to try something new and different, to keep going and to enjoy your successes. Passion keeps us engaged in fulfilling our values.

Without a connection to our values our passions can either become muted, leading to depression, or they can run wild and not accomplish much.

We can generally be in three states around our values:

1. Your values are the basis of your passion – if you want to have more excitement day after day, then nurture the connection between your values and your passion

2. You are not sure what your values are, and might feel a lot of ambivalence in your life. Clarifying your values will help you feel more passion and motivation.

3. When you're out of alignment, you set up an internal conflict. The conflicting beliefs you are holding in tension will undermine your efforts at success.

Of course you can be in and out of alignment with different values at different times. Here are some examples:

1. When I'm writing, or training or coaching, I'm very much in alignment with my values of helping people and working in my genius. It helps me to be in a 'flow' state and for the work to come easily to me.

2. When I'm procrastinating, I might not really understand the values that I'm expressing, and it might be a great opportunity to explore that.

3. When I'm eating a huge lunch with a big fat chocolate tart for dessert, I'm in alignment with my values for satisfaction, but out of alignment with my values for being healthy and balancing my blood sugar.

Losing our Connection to our Motivation

Our connection with our values is often lost in the daily grind of nit-picky issues and humdrum operations. We get distracted by bright shiny objects and meetings and emails grind us down until we start to lose the motivation and the vision of why we started this whole thing anyway.

Where is the spark? Why did you start your business? What got you to where you are now?

It probably wasn't the money. Of course money is great, it can pay for a nicer house, cool vacations, your kids' education. It might be part of your 'why', but it's probably not the only part. Maybe it's an extension – what can money do for you? Will it buy you freedom from debt, or the ability to travel, or will you finally be able to have nicer things?

Maybe your 'why' is about changing the world? Leaving a legacy, being something bigger, better, newer and more helpful... Maybe you want to help people.

Maybe you want the excitement of being a part of something new, or building something yourself from scratch.

Maybe you don't really know what your core values are. If not, I strongly suggest that you spend an hour or two working with the exercise at the end of this chapter. This will help you to get a clearer sense of your values and their connection to your vision and goals.

What Gets in the Way of Living in Your Values?

Even after you can clearly articulate your value system, it's easy to get caught up in the day-to-day, losing sight of the big picture, which can lead to feeling unmotivated. If you've already defined your values, you can recall and re-access them and quickly become re-motivated.

If you haven't defined your values and see a clear path between your values and what you are working toward then you might become unmotivated. This is particularly difficult. Being an entrepreneur is hard! Staying connected to your values and passion can help to ease the way.

I was talking with a client yesterday who felt stuck. She has a big, and achievable, goal and she's not doing any work on it at all. When I asked her about it, she shared that she feels like it's too much, and she's not sure it will succeed, so she doesn't work on it at all! It seemed like her enthusiasm was dampened and scattered. Once we really got clear about her values and her outcome, she was able to reconnect with her passion and motivation and get moving on it.

Having a clear connection to values is a new way of thinking for most people. Most people are caught up in intermediate goals, thinking that will be enough to propel them forward. When they first have a new project or business idea, or are sold on an idea, they are connected with their motivation (or at least they are enthusiastic about the motivation and vision that has been presented by the person who sold the idea). They might have done a course, or had a great conversation, or had an idea for a business and they get dizzy with the possibility of it all.

They are fired up and excited, and they start working at their new idea. They start working up a plan, and slowly it dawns that this is going to involve some hard work. That's ok – all businesses involve some element of hard work, but then they get caught up in the doing and lose connection with why they are doing it. They start to become disconnected from the motivation that inspired them to get started in the first place. They get caught in the weeds.

Being an Entrepreneur is HARD

This is often more difficult because being an entrepreneur is HARD. Some of the aspects of the entrepreneurial journey make it particularly difficult, including:

1. The ambiguity of the decisions we need to make
2. Self-confidence and building mastery
3. The number of new things we need to learn
4. Handling failure

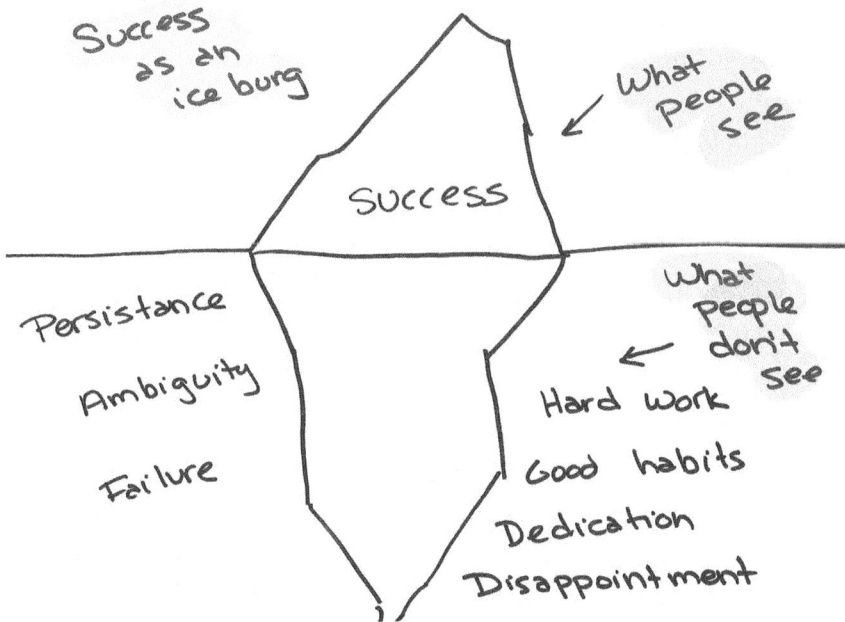

Success as an iceburg

What people see

Success

What people don't see

Persistance
Ambiguity
Failure

Hard work
Good habits
Dedication
Disappointment

Ambiguity

A lot of stories about entrepreneurs tend to cut out the messy stuff. They often go something like this: I had a great idea. I took it to market. Huge success!

The truth of being an entrepreneur is that there is no simple trajectory. There are no straight lines, and there is a huge amount of uncertainty.

In the corporate or government world, things tend to be fairly clear. There are regulations, policies and procedures, KPIs (Key Performance Indicators – more on this in chapter 4) and deliverables, all designed to make sure everyone knows what they're doing.

Being an entrepreneur means living in a permanent state of ambiguity. On one hand you need to have clear direction and vision and the clarity and enthusiasm to bring others along on your vision (clients, investors, employees). On the other hand, you need to be constantly evaluating what you are doing, assessing if this is the right direction. The art of the successful entrepreneur is being able to hold these two (or more) ideas in tension and getting on with it anyway.

When you have a clear sense of your values and reconnect with your vision and your "why" – the whole reason you started this business anyway – on a regular basis, then it helps you to manage the ambiguity and learn to survive and even thrive in a world where you sometimes need to act a whole lot more certain about the "right" answer than you actually are.

The good news is that this skill can be learned. Successful entrepreneurs cultivate this skill and embrace uncertainty. Having a clear vision helps. Knowing that failure and uncertainty is all part of the process is essential. Just as this program can bring you into a state of mind that helps you to imagine yourself into success and integrate this into your life, the same techniques can be used to get comfortable with ambiguity, and even failure, and be totally ok with that.

Failure, Pivot & Perseverance

Entrepreneurs need to get really comfortable with the potential for failure. As mentioned above, we need to hold in our consciousness both the drive for success, and the potential for failure, and be able to bounce back. We need to learn to view what we would typically call 'failure' as 'feedback'. When we talk about our operating system, we need to re-code the way we look at the outcome of our efforts. It's actually a complex skill because for every 'failure' there is an option to re-evaluate the business and make any of the following choices:

1. Learn from it and try a different approach. When a reporter asked, "How did it feel to fail 1,000 times?" Thomas Edison replied, "I didn't fail 1,000 times. The light bulb was an invention with 1,000 steps."
2. Pivot – use the same ideas, but in a different way. For example, twitter started as an application to allow people to subscribe to podcasts. With the rise of iTunes they saw the writing on the wall and re-purposed their technology as a social platform.
3. Cut your losses – stop the business and put your efforts into some other endeavour

Unfortunately, a lot of people focus on what they are creating rather than why they are creating it. This can make them inflexible in how they think about their business, and how they approach problems. It changes the way they look at failure and how they approach recovery.

Here are some of my favorite quotes about ways to look at failure.

> *"Our greatest glory is not in never falling but in rising every time we fall." ~ Confucius*

> *"Failing is one of the greatest arts in the world. One fails toward success." ~ Charles Kettering*

"Failure provides the opportunity to begin again, more intelligently." ~ Henry Ford

"The fastest way to succeed is to double your failure rate." ~ Thomas Watson Sr.

"Flops are a part of life's menu and I've never been a girl to miss out on any of the courses." ~ Rosalind Russell

"Every great cause is born from repeated failures and from imperfect achievements." ~ Maria Montessori

As entrepreneurs, we need to remember that every step that we take is a great step even though sometimes we take a step that isn't going to work for us and isn't going to have the results that we want. When that happens we learn and we keep going. So one of the strengths of being an entrepreneur is being able to work with feedback (failure).

One way to handle negative feedback is to get grounded in yourself, and reconnect with your values. This is one of the keys to resilience. When you take the time in those difficult moments to reconnect with your vision and your values, it can give you a new perspective on the moment, and help you to persevere.

Learning New Things Is Hard

As an entrepreneur, you are learning a lot of new skills. Skills that help you navigate your business, skills that you need to relate to people and bring them into your business, and skills that help to navigate the new ways of thinking that you are developing.

Learning new things is hard, and it takes a lot of time

Most of the time when we are working at a 'job', we learn things incrementally. We start with knowing 95% of what we need to be successful, and then learn the other 5% as we go along. Also, we're generally learning 1–2 new things at a time.

As an entrepreneur, there is often a lot more that we don't know. We might need to learn:

- Sales
- Marketing
- Accounting
- Research
- Business & Legal
- Negotiations
- Product / service specific skills

Whew! That's a lot!

Research has shown that learning happens faster when we are building on a foundation of things we already know. The connections between neurons that already exist in our brain light up more readily when approaching a task with some familiar elements than they do when the task is completely unfamiliar.

It is the skills that are completely outside of our experience that take the most cognitive effort.

How does this relate to values and vision? Again, when things get hard is the time to reconnect with your 'why', to reconnect with your motivation and accept that 'yes – this is hard, and there's a really good reason I'm doing it'.

Self-confidence and building mastery

I watched this really really interesting TED talk (Technology, Entertainment, Design) about how to develop self-confidence. It really resonated for me because the gentleman talked about how self-confidence is developed through experience.

The basic model around confidence is that we feel more confident with things that we've done a lot and been successful at.

So it may be that the first time you pitch somebody to sell your product to them, you might not feel very confident, you might not really know what you're doing. On the other hand, the 50th time or the hundredth time or the 500th time after you've had some success in it and you've tried different things and found out what works for you, you're going to have more confidence.

So the point here is that confidence is often linked to your experience – how many times you've done it and how many times you've been successful.

Mastery and self-confidence is a traditional motivator, and one that we often don't feel as entrepreneurs. Sometimes this means we need to go back to our beliefs and look at the limiting belief "I'm not good enough", and sometimes this just means we need to learn new things. Sometimes it means we need to get those good feelings of confidence from imagining the values that will be fulfilled when we have done the work and fulfilled on our vision.

Values and Productivity

One difference between busy people and productive people is that productive people have a vision. That doesn't mean they have a vision of running a successful and lucrative business, or being an effective manager – that's not enough. They have a vision of WHY they want to run a successful and lucrative business or be an amazing manager.

When you are not clear on your endpoint, it can be hard to focus on what you should be doing in the short-term. If you have 15 tasks to do today, you can focus on the easiest, the hardest, or the one you haven't done before. But none of those decisions are informed by what will have the highest value in achieving your lifetime goal. Taking the time to zero in on your lifetime values and linking them to what you need to do to get there makes the smallest, everyday decision that much easier. It's like taking a photo in nature. Do you want to focus on the bird or the flower? The leaf or the horizon? First you decide what you want to emphasise, and you zoom in on that. Suddenly, everything that is important in your day comes into sharp focus.

A lot of goal setting and life planning in the past revolved around five or ten year plans. These plans have a purpose, but they only make sense when that span of time is connected to your life goals – your values. As an entrepreneur, it can be hard to have a clear sense of where you will be in five years, or even one year. Sometimes you'll start out in one direction and then four months later be doing something completely different. The terrain is uncertain and ever-changing – a new piece of technology could come along and change the whole game. One thing you can do is to be clear about the why of what you are doing.

For some people that vision might mean having financial security, and for others it might mean creating a business that helps people. Whatever their vision is, they are clear about what it is and it informs every decision they make in their working day.

Successful people connect with their vision every day. This means that when they wake up, they know exactly what they need to do to move their vision forward. Vision is what inspires them and gives them direction. Vision is what sets their agenda and gets them focusing on the few key actions that will best serve that vision each day.

Productive people look at a list of tasks and ask the question 'what will move my vision forward today?'. Their lists are short. Busy people have long 'to do' lists and many more tasks in the back of their minds to be done. Productive people have just a few high quality, high productivity and high lifetime value tasks that they focus on at any one time.

Other ways productive people use vision

Vision is what gives productive people the confidence and clarity to set their own agenda, and not be steered off course by other people's priorities. They have a clear sense of direction and purpose, and having a clear direction – a clear vision – is the key to supercharging your productivity.

Vision also helps productive people to say 'no' more often. Busy people say 'yes' a lot. In our society, we are trained to say yes, and it's hard to say no. Productive people use their clarity of vision to say 'no'. One of the most important pieces of advice that Warren Buffet – one of the most successful investors in the world – gives is the importance of saying 'no'. In fact, he says he has only made a few investments in his life! Saying no to other people's agendas is what successful people are really really good at, and the confidence to do that comes from their clear sense of direction and their values.

CHAPTER 4

The Success Roadmap: Growth Hacking 3.0

"A goal without a plan is just a wish."
~ Antoine de Saint-Exupéry

In 2012 I was running a publishing company (which I loved) and doing project consulting in Silicon Valley. My life was really great, and there was a new idea I wanted to explore – creating an eCommerce store.

The challenge was that I was already working far more than full time in my existing businesses.

Or so I thought...

Here's how a typical Tuesday used to look: get up – check email – put out fires... go to meetings... help out the team...

I was letting other people set my agenda. I went to useless meetings that zapped my motivation. I would hear the email ding, and my concentration would be shot as I rushed to see what was in my inbox.

It was a habit, and my focus and attention were constantly being pulled in different directions. I would try to take care of the 'important' things (like eating well and exercising) around the 'urgent' things (like email and meetings).

I didn't eat well, I didn't exercise, I didn't relax – and I still wasn't getting anything done!

At the end of the day I felt frustrated because I looked back on my day and didn't really have anything meaningful to show for it. I hadn't moved the needle forward at all!

It was weird because first off, I'm a certified project manager, so I help people succeed for a living, also I had been studying productivity and time management for years – always taking the latest course, learning how to use a new checklist or planner. None of it was helping.

One day (while I was goofing off looking at the internet) I saw an article on how CEOs and high-level executives manage their businesses.

There's a secret that they have that we don't. What I read stunned me – it was so simple, and completely different from anything I had ever learned.

What makes them so much more productive is that they don't try to manage time. They manage themselves. They manage their beliefs, their motivation and their tasks.

I realized when I was trying to 'manage time' I was going from the outside in. I was trying to use external means to fix an internal problem.

The truth is that time keeps going – whether we manage it or not. All we can manage is ourselves.

I realized that to live the life that I really wanted – to have freedom and success – I needed to take control of my life and my business. I only have a certain amount of time in every day.

Getting Intentional about Your Business

Lost time is never found again. ~ Benjamin Franklin

I've talked to a lot of entrepreneurs and business people who are struggling and they tell me "Well, I don't exactly know what I should do each day. I don't know what the most important tasks are". So they don't do anything! Or they do things that don't really move their businesses forward and then feel frustrated.

Often they are not connected to their values, so they don't have a clear idea of why they are working so hard for such meagre results. They know what they don't want, and not what they do want. They don't have control of their life or their business.

In the next section we're going to talk about how to create a Success Roadmap so that you will wake up every day knowing exactly what you need to do to move your needle forward.

Why do you need a Success Roadmap?

Being busy does not always mean real work. The object of all work is production or accomplishment and to either of these ends there must be forethought, system, planning, intelligence, and honest purpose, as well as perspiration. Seeming to do is not doing. ~ Thomas A. Edison

Learning how to plan is one of the critical success factors to being a successful entrepreneur. If you don't plan, then you don't really know if you are spending your time on the tasks that are the best and fastest way to your goals. You might be doing the things that are easy rather than your highest value tasks that move you closer to your goals, to your vision.

Here's a little story that resonates for many entrepreneurs...

One night, a police officer was walking his beat and came across a man on his hands and knees in a pool of light under a lamp post. The officer asked the man what he was doing. The man replied "I'm looking for my keys". The officer joined the search and, after some time, they both straightened up, empty handed. "Are you sure you lost them here?" he said. "No", said the man, "I lost them over there, but the light's better here".

This is a cautionary tale about focusing on the easy task and not the most important tasks. The challenge is that often the most important tasks are difficult.

When you get to the point where you have a team or staff (which you may already have) planning and clarity is going to be critical to helping them understand how they can best support the company and earn their pay.

Challenge with Entrepreneurial Project Planning

Let's say that you know exactly what you want. You have it very well defined. Then the task is just getting there.

When you work in the corporate world, generally the path to success is pretty well defined. It's been trodden by people before you. There are training manuals, managers, and other employees to guide you. There are project managers and staff to support you. It's like driving on a highway, the road is clear, paved with well marked rest stops, exits and viewpoints.

When you become an entrepreneur, often the path to success is not a clear path. As an entrepreneur, 'getting from Point A to Point B' is rarely going to be a straight, smooth path. It's going to be more like hacking your way through a jungle with a machete.

You might run into a ravine.

You might run into quicksand.

And you might need to figure out how to sharpen your machete in order to keep going.

You will be confronting these different challenges without anyone telling you whether you're going in the right direction and whether you can even get to point B from there.

Now, this isn't true for everyone. If you are working with a partner, coach or mentor (and I really advocate this if it's at all possible), or if you are working in a field where other people have already created a working model, then following the model or taking the course or getting a coach or getting a mentor can save you thousands and thousands of dollars and years of your life.

For example, when I built my eCommerce store I didn't have a whole lot of knowledge about how to start an online store. I was lucky because I found a step-by-step model to follow and had a mentor who had already done it and been successful.

I had also already done some of the tasks involved before. For me, managing an eCommerce store used a lot of skills I had developed in other businesses. That, together with the step-by-step model, allowed me to systemize the model quickly and focus on my highest value tasks and outsource the rest of them.

I started with self-confidence in 70% of the tasks that I was doing, so the challenging bits were not so challenging. I was able to approach the development of my new business confident in my ability to do most of the things I needed to do.

Because of this, and together with the other skills I'm talking about in this book, I was able build a high six figure business that doubled every year for three years.

On the other hand, many people I've met, even people who are building an eCommerce store try to do the whole thing themselves. They struggle to forge a new path rather than taking the path that others have created and making modifications to suit their businesses.

Whether you are deciding to create a completely new path with your business, or build on an existing model, the Success Roadmap can help you to reach your goals in the quickest and most effective way possible.

The Success Roadmap

You must learn from the mistakes of others. You can't possibly live long enough to make them all yourself.
~ Sam Levenson

The Success Roadmap is a culmination of my 10 years of research into how highly successful businesses work plus my own experience and what I've learned from coaching business leaders.

1. Have a clear vision of where you are going.
2. Focus on working on your business rather than being in your business
3. Keep your mind focused on the goal and let go of mind clutter
4. Prioritize project planning and focus on the highest value projects
5. Test your market and your ideas as quickly as possible
6. Focus on the highest value tasks
7. Measure and assess your progress regularly

In this chapter you are going to learn the components of the Success Roadmap and how to apply it to your business.

1. Have a clear vision of where you are going.

If you completed the exercises in the previous chapter, you will now have a clear sense of your vision and your values, and a clear connection between your values and where you want to go.

Now, when you wake up every day you're going to be motivated because you know what you will be working on. You're really excited about what you're going to create and what that's going to do for you in your life.

If you haven't completed the exercises, go here and do them (http://www.angelicobooks.com/success)

2. Focus on working on their business rather than being in their business

You've probably heard this before. Let's dig a little further into it.

What does it mean?

Working on your business means taking a big step back and looking at the whole picture. Often as entrepreneurs we wear a lot of different hats, we may do marketing, sales, production, accounting, take out the trash… All of this is 'in' our business. At least once a week we need to step back and look at the big picture – the entire hat rack (☺). We want to check to make sure we're going in the right direction.

Why is it important?

It's important because things change. Sometimes we get so focused on specific tasks that we don't notice that they may be leading us in the wrong direction. Sometimes something goes wrong and we make a course correction, and then we need to step back and see how that fits into the big picture.

How can you do it?

This depends on how big your team is. When I'm working with solopreneurs I suggest that they allocate a specific time every week to focus ON their business. I do it for about 2 hours a week, and the team leaders in each of my companies do it for about 2 weeks [??] as well. In this time you might would:

– Look at metrics

– Assess themselves against goals

– Do course corrections

– Plan out the strategic priorities for the following week.

As your team grows, you spend less and less time actually DOING the work and more time managing it.

3. Keep your mind focused on the goal and let go of mind clutter

I suggest that the first thing you do in your allocated weekly or daily strategic time is to empty out your brain. This will help you get everything out of your head and onto paper. Most people find that this simple exercise helps them clear off their mental desk.

It's almost like your mental desk gets piled high with clutter during the week, or your computer memory gets filled up. The task is to get all your clear the clutter and move it from whispers in your mind, to concrete words on a piece of paper so you can make decisions about it. Here's the exercise:

Part 1: Brain Dump

1. Pull out a piece of paper (yes, paper!) and a pen. If you really want to use a computer then open a textpad (and I do suggest pen and paper)

2. Write out anything that comes to mind – just write out everything in your head. Start with free writing for 10 minutes, then you might look at some specific questions:

   a. What do I need "to do"

   b. What do I feel like I "owe" people

   c. Are there any outstanding expectations or tasks that are nagging me (like making an appointment with the dentist, or getting the dry cleaning done)

    d. Anything that is bothering you – that you are worrying about or that you might be telling yourself, like "I'm not getting enough done", or "I'm worried about…"

    e. Past unfinished business

3. Let anything come – like brainstorming, leave any judgement at the door and just write.

Part 2: Decide

"Whenever you see a successful business, someone once made a courageous decision." ~ Peter F. Drucker

Now let's take this huge list of things and make it more organized.

1. Go through list and put a checkmark by everything that is outside your control and star next to everything that is in your control and put them in a list.

2. Start with the checkmarks. Look at each thing and make a conscious decision about whether you are going to try to control it, or if you are willing to let it go.

3. Now move on to the things that are starred. For each of these, make one of the following decisions:

    a. It is not important, and I'm going to consciously let it go

    b. I'm going to delegate this to someone else, and then add the name of who it will be delegated to

    c. I'm going to do this later – then add it to your calendar for a later date

    d. This is critical to do this week.

Ideally there are not more than 10 tasks on the "d" list and they are well-defined. If not, consider whether you can move them to any of the other lists.

Now that you have de-cluttered your mind, you are ready to focus on creating a Success Roadmap.

4. *Prioritize project planning and focus on the highest value projects*

> *"Planning is bringing the future into the present so that you can do something about it now."* ~ Alan Lakein

Now that you have a clear sense of your goals, have committed to working ON your business at least a few hours a week, and have cleared your mind of clutter you are ready to create a Success Roadmap, a clear path of how to get from where you are to where you want to go.

Let's talk about the nitty-gritty. What is a project plan and how do you create one?

A project plan is a clear, step-by-step plan that takes you from where you are, to the results that you want. Project plans are documents that help you understand the specific tasks, dependencies and measurements of success. A project plan can be a simple spreadsheet with some notes, or a huge document. The goal is to create a project plan that is just the right size and complexity to support your business goals.

The first step is to look at your business and to determine the projects that need to be completed.

What is a project?

It is a planned set of interrelated tasks to be executed over a fixed period and within certain cost and other limitations. (businessdictionary.com)

A project is a clear path to reaching a goal. Creating a project plan takes a big goal and turns it into a clearly defined set of tasks with measurable inputs and outputs.

There are going to be many different projects within your business and that can be overwhelming.

When you break it down you can see specifically what needs to be done, what needs to be done by you, what skills, tools or systems you might need to support you, and what you can outsource or delegate.

A project is done just once, and a process is something that continues over time.

For example, setting up your bookkeeping is a project, whereas doing your monthly bookkeeping is a process. Setting up your legal structure is a project. Gathering tax receipts is a project, and paying your taxes is a process. Organizing your marketing system is a project and, once you have it set up and running, you have a process.

Growing your business is a collection of projects.

Defining what projects you have in your business is a project, and it will be a key project to start with. Some big projects can be divided into smaller projects, or a series of projects. Some projects may have sub-projects.

How Do You Define Your Projects?

To define your projects, do something similar to the Clearing the Clutter process.

Write down everything that you're working on, and write down everything that you want to accomplish. Write down everything that you think needs to be done to be successful in your business.

This would be everything from the logistical tasks like your accounting and legal to marketing and creating your product or service.

Write it all down and then start to group it.

Generally, things will fall into fairly well-defined groups. These groups may be projects, or they may be a main project with subprojects. In my mind, a project should not take more than a month to complete. If it takes more than a month to complete, then it probably should be broken up into smaller projects.

For example, I managed an R&D project to create an industrial valve for a medical manufacturing company. That was an 18 month project, so a project can be longer than a month. In this case, a series of sub-projects helped to keep track of milestones and give a sense of achievement at each step.

If you have a team, you will also ask everybody on your team to write down all the things they're working on.

Project Example

Let's look at defining your sales process as a project.

Your sales process might be online or in person.

Creating a simple online sales funnel would be a project, and each of the individual tasks below is large enough to be a sub-project:

1. *Define Your Lead source*: Facebook, Instagram, Email, Joint Ventures, other
2. *Website*, including opt-in page or some way to collect email address
3. *Website Opt-in Bribe* – or some reason for someone to give you an email address
4. *Email* – set up your email management system
5. *Initial low price offering* – the initial low-cost product that a potential customer might purchase

6. *Email series* – the marketing that helps the customer start to know, like, and trust you

7. *Phone call* or customer purchase of your product (assuming you have another project running where you created your product)

Setting up a face-to-face sales funnel might include:

1. Lead source – conferences, networking events, speaking engagements, referrals

2. Elevator pitch, or connecting script – way to get someone engaged with you and give you a business card

3. Contact management system

4. Product offerings (again, optimally starting with a low cost offer)

5. Follow up plan

6. Sale

I'm stepping you through this example because everybody does sales and the sales process is a critical one in the business.

Your sales funnel is a major project, and this might be broken down into sub-projects. For example, creating your low cost offer might be a sub-project. Creating your plan for approaching networking events is another sub-project. The next one might be creating your website. Each of these projects has a set of tasks, which we'll get into shortly.

Once you have a big list of projects, now it's important to focus on your top 2–5 projects. How do you know which ones to focus on?

The goal is to determine the Highest Value Projects

These projects will have the highest value of return in the lowest period of time.

These are the projects that will help you "prove" the concept of your business or your approach, and maximize income as early in the business as possible.

We use the model called 'growth hacking' similar to the concept of 'lean startup' – putting something together quickly so you can get it out into the market and get some feedback. You don't want to spend six months putting together one part of your final offering and then have it rejected by the market. We're going to talk more about growth hacking later on the chapter.

Choosing the Highest Value Projects

How do you define highest value? Your highest value activities are those which are going to have the

- biggest impact on the customer, and the
- biggest long-term impact

These projects are going to be different based on the stage of your company. Below are some ideas of what may be critical projects based on your company stage.

STAGE **1** – Startup: At the very beginning of the company you want to test the idea and get initial feedback from the market as quickly as possible. Here the projects that are most important tend to be around getting customers and managing cash.

STAGE **2** – Survival: At this point you have initial customers and sales, the idea has been confirmed, and the task is to grow sales and build out the business offerings. Here the most important projects tend to be around sales and delivery.

STAGE **3** – Systemize: Now the business is growing both in sales and in team members. Now it is critical to start to systematize, create an operations manual and start to transition into a potentially sellable asset.

STAGE 4 – Evolve: New managers are brought in, the systems are stable, and the owner has a few options, a) to step into a higher level of leadership, b) hire in senior management and leave, or c) hire in senior management and continue to work in an R&D position or in a position of maximal value. In this stage the projects are around making the transition to a long term management structure.

STAGE 5 – Stable: At a certain point the business is established and gets into a stable state, now the goals are to leverage the stability in order to innovate and find new ways to continue to grow.

	Urgent	Not Urgent
Important	Some customer calls Crisis management	Planning Strategy Review
Not Important	Interruptions Most email	Checking Facebook Busy work

Important and Urgent Projects

As you are working through your projects and items, and the items your teams have sent through, think about them in terms of what's important and what's urgent.

What's the difference between important and urgent?

Steven Covey, the guru of time management and effectiveness, gave us the following urgent vs important matrix. It's a useful way of mapping tasks so that you are focusing on your highest impact items first, and parking or delegating things that aren't crucial to your immediate objective. It's a really useful way to get clear on what's in front of you.

The Priority Matrix

Prioritizing projects can also be helpful in terms of getting a clear sense of focus. You can do this by creating criteria for weighting the importance or urgency of each task and tasking your team (or yourself) accordingly.

Criteria might include:

- Required – Is it required to meet legal or regulatory guidelines?
- Strategic Value – Does it align with our overall strategy and mission?
- Ease – How hard will it be?
- Financial Benefit – When this project is done, how much will it contribute financially?
- Cost – How much will the project cost?
- Resource Impact – How much will it impact resources (people, equipment)?

Work with your team to agree on scores for each project so that the ratings are agreed. In a small team, this process can also help to clarify tasks and processes.

The goal is to identify the top 3–5 projects and focus your resources on those projects.

What I often find is that Entrepreneurs get caught up in projects that are not that important, then they wonder why they are not having the progress that they desire. Once you start focusing on the right projects, you'll start to see clearer results from your efforts.

5. *Test market and ideas as quickly as possible*

Last week I had a consultation with Henree, an executive in London. He had been a very successful executive for 20 years, and now was starting a training company to provide training and consulting to corporate executives. He was feeling very frustrated because his business was not moving as quickly as he wanted it to, and he was running out of money.

I asked him about his product. It was an online training course and he was getting bogged down in course creation. He wanted the course to be perfect before he shared his ideas with anyone, and at this rate it would take 2 years for him to get there. This was 2 years of R&D before he even tested the idea to see if anyone would be interested in purchasing it!

This is a story I hear over and over, and, unfortunately, often times the entrepreneur spends a lot of time, money and effort creating something, only to find out that they can't sell it, or that in order to sell it they need to create it in a slightly different way. All that time, money and focus is wasted.

The solution is the Minimum Viable Product. I first learned about this concept from the book Lean Startup by Eric Ries.

Your minimum viable product (MVP) has just enough features to allow you to get it out to potential customers and see if customers will pay you money for it, but not so much development that you will have to go backwards, or have risked too much time or capital.

Ideally, a MVP has the minimum number of features that will attract the customers you want and serve their needs. The minimum features you will be clear on from your market research, and any additional product development will happen later. You can then gather feedback from those customers and use it to add features later, without having to strip back any unnecessary features from the first release.

So, for example, with Henree his Minimum Viable Product might be either a 1 hour training, to test whether people would purchase the training at all, or doing the full training, but doing it live so he could test the market without having to do massive production.

Minimum Viable Product Honing

In reviewing the diagram below (based on Expressive Product Design by Fred Voorhorst) shows that Minimum Viable Product can be completely different depending on what it is that you are trying to test.

For example, if Henree wants to test if his content is a good match for his audience, he might sell face to face training. If he wants to test if people will watch his training online, he might provide a smaller set of training for testing.

The goal is to define is the absolute minimum that you need to create in order to get to test your idea and to get feedback.

In The Sprint Book, Jake Knapp, John Zeratsky and Braden Kowitz talk about exactly that, taking this cycle and making it even shorter, and doing it in one week. They run through a five-day process to take an idea from 'just an idea' all the way to user testing.

It's a rigorous ride through that process, and I would be happy to coach you through it if you're interested.

Most people, though, will use the standard MVP process.

In working with Lisa on her book, the question was, "what is the smallest book with the least content that you can publish and start to get feedback on?"

And how to publish that book in such a way that you're not printing 10 million copies before you have some feedback on it and find out whether people really want it?

Let's look at how you can use this process in your life.

If you're doing information marketing or if you're selling a product online, what is the smallest sales flow you can create (or the smallest product you can create) that will give you a chance to test whether people are going to purchase your product?

If you're creating a service, how do you test it on a few customers using a flow that's as similar to your final flow as possible before automating the final flow?

And, if you're selling a product, is there a way to get some prototypes into the market? Is there a way to test the product with its end-users?

What are the fewest number of features that you need on that product in order to get it out into the market and get it tested?

Once you've tested your minimum viable product, then the next question is how can you expand that minimum viable product to add more features so that people will buy more?

So if you have a book, how do you turn that into a course?

If you have a service how do you add additional services to your basic service and up-sell people?

If you have a product, are there other things that you can add to that product to make it more valuable to the customer? How can you build a product range where each product builds on the other?

As a productivity consultant I often help executives finish their books and get them to market. Recently, I worked with Lisa, an aspiring travel writer who was completely overwhelmed. First off, she considers herself "not a writer, but an adventurer".

She felt like it was an impossible task, and she didn't know where to start.

First I asked Lisa what was the absolute least amount of content she need to have in the book in order to get meaningful feedback from real customers (beyond friends and family). What's the minimum that you need to put out in order to feel satisfied and test the market and see if people are going to buy it?

Just asking that question helped her relax because she was able to take something that felt very amorphous, large and confusing and hone in on it and make it very concrete.

When it's concrete you then you can make a clear, well-defined action to move it forward. It's very difficult to move an amorphous idea forward.

Lisa decided that her MVP was:

1. The lead up – the why behind the adventure
2. All the funny mini stories

3. A bigger message/journey woven through the smaller stories
4. Some practical information about the places she visited
5. A map of her travels
6. A few photos or hand-drawn illustrations

Having this MVP defined allowed us to take the next step to create a Success Map.

6. Create a Well-Defined Project Plan

> *"Give me six hours to chop down a tree and I will spend the first four sharpening the axe." ~ Abraham Lincoln*

The first step is to take the time to plan – our first step in working together is to work with the big picture and the questions is: "what exactly you are trying to do? how we can break this big, seemingly impossible, task into something that is well-defined with bite sized pieces?".

When I was working with Lisa she knew exactly what she was trying to accomplish and when we did the MVP (above) we broke out the components. Components are not a plan. The next step is to get even clearer about what is the minimum measure of success.

So we ask questions to determine the detailed plans.

Defining questions in this case might be:

1. How long do you think the 'lead-up and why' needs to be? What are some things that need to be covered?
2. How many 'funny mini stories'? How long is each one?
3. What are the main messages and themes?
4. What type of practical information? Is this a checklist or a travel manual?
5. Is this a custom map, a clipart map or a google map?

6. What value are the photos and illustrations going to give, and are you willing to forgo them, or do them as a second phase?

The next step is to start to get it granular. You may think your project is well defined, and once you start breaking it down into manageable chunks you can start to make it really granular.

Ideally, each task should take 4–12 hours to complete.

So for the book project that granularity might go down to a detailed outline with specific titles for the mini-stories, and an outline of the introduction and the practical information.

You want your task to be granular, but not excruciatingly, mind-numbingly, granular.

With Lisa, the plan we created laid out what needs to be done each week, and she could see a clear path from her point A (having had amazing adventures and stories in her mind), to her point B (a completed book of her adventures).

If the task becomes too granular, then it takes more time to update the project plan than it's worth.

A task might take two or three days and that will go in the plan, but chances are you're not going to put in a task that takes an hour, unless it's setting up a meeting to get sign-off from a client or from a client representative.

The next step is define the timeline needed to complete each piece. Each task in your project plan needs to have a start date and an end date.

If you don't know your dates, make an estimate and track it so you can see how accurate you are. Over time, you will get better at estimating task lengths, and estimating tasks is an important skill for an entrepreneur.

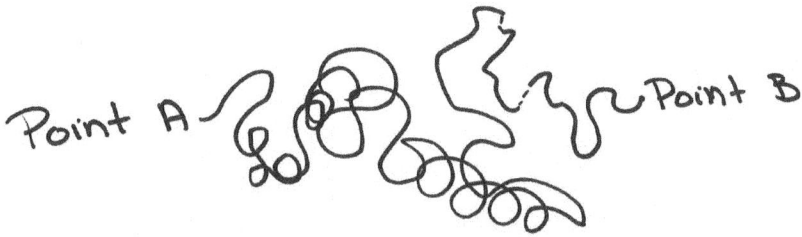

Point A —> Point B with lots of convoluted lines

Point A —> Point B with a black box

Point A —> Point B with a straight line with tick marks on it (like a ruler)

Other questions to ponder as you create your project plan:

1. What resources are you going to need, is it something you'll do all yourself, is it something you're going to involve other people in, or are you going to need specific technology?

2. If you need other people to complete your sub-projects, now is a good time to check in on their timelines, see if they are available and what their cost might be.

3. Is there anything you need to learn in order to do this project? Do you know how to do all the pieces already or do you need to learn them? Do you need to find another resource who already knows how to do them who can do them for you?

4. Who is responsible for this project? If you have a team, you can delegate responsibility for certain tasks to other people. I delegate a lot to my team, and when I write my project plan I put in the names of who is responsible.

5. How will you know if it's done? What is it supposed to look like when it's done? Sometimes that's clear, and sometimes you have to clarify that and put some more definition around it. Key performance indicators are how you will measure success.

Key performance indicators (KPIs). KPIs are, unfortunately, not in most 'traditional' project plans. KPIs are particularly important for entrepreneurs. Entrepreneurs don't usually have thousands or millions of dollars to spend on making mistakes. They need to find out what works quickly and on the minimum possible budget.

What is a Key Performance Indicator (KPI)?

A KPI is measurable, and gives a value to how effectively a person, product or business is at achieving its objectives. KPIs are used to help businesses track progress against targets. A critical part of growth hacking is to add KPIs to your project planning.

Let's continue with sales and marketing as an example of how to use KPIs. Here are some examples of KPIs for an online sales funnel:

1. Number of social media engagements. For example, on Facebook that might be the number of likes or number of comments.

2. Number of downloads.

3. Number of people on your email list

Examples of face-to-face marketing

1. Number of business cards collected

2. Number of opportunities to follow up

3. Number of sales of specific products

4. Number of customers

For Research and Development

1. Income

2. Costs

3. Prototypes

4. New products to market

Every project in your business should have some KPIs so that you will you know if each project is successful.

Final review

Once you've sketched out the whole project and put the information into either the Success Roadmap or into your project planning software, review it one last time.

The question to ask yourself at this stage is "Okay, which of the things in this project are a 'must have', and what in this project is a 'nice to have'?"

Even though you've done this analysis already, do one final pass with this question in mind. This is your chance to ask yourself, "Can we hone this down even more?" It's also a great time to go out to some friends or colleagues, and get some feedback. A word of warning – only do this with people who you think support your success.

Your project plan will guide your success. Most successful entrepreneurs (or their teams) review the project plan every week and make adjustments as needed.

The next step is to actually do the work.

You might spend between a few hours and a few days planning out your business.

Then, each week, you need to check your project plan and, again, focus on the top two or three tasks that you want to get done each week.

What I've learned is that when you try to do more than two or three tasks each week, often none of them get done. This circles back to the highest lifetime value tasks linking back to your highest lifetime value goals.

For me, my highest value tasks (the ones that make me the most money and allow me to have the biggest impact in my business) are around creating products and finding ways to connect my products with the right buyers.

Those are the things that are going to create the highest value in my life and the lives of the people I want to support. While accounting has to be done, and I definitely make sure that it's done, I don't do it myself. I do, however, make sure that I am focused every week on how I get my message out there more and how I increase or improve my products.

Every week, have one to three well-defined tasks that you're planning on accomplishing that week. At the end of the week evaluate them and ask, "did I accomplish these? If not, what got in the way? Did I take too much on? Do I need to delegate tasks? Or do I need to make them smaller, the tasks?" If you don't accomplish them, potential issues might be:

- the task was too big
- it wasn't the highest value task
- you got blocked somewhere in doing it – maybe you're out of your Success Zone (see Chapter 2)

Be absolutely clear about what your primary tasks are going to be this week, and the primary tasks of your team.

To get them done, put the tasks into your schedule.

For a long time I was not a big believer in putting tasks into schedules. It felt too restrictive to me for my style of productive working. Then I read an article that convinced me that tasks are more likely to get done if they're in a schedule. I tried it out and was surprised at how well it works!

Now we can have a long conversation about tasks and scheduling and I could write a whole book just about this.

The way I have worked with this method (and it's working very well for me), is to put the tasks in my schedule, but always give priority to the things that are your highest value tasks and are of the highest creativity.

Let's say that it's Thursday morning and you are scheduled to work on your accounting project. You wake up on Thursday morning and you say, "Wow, I am feeling really creative, I really want to work on this other high-value creative task."

In that case, by all means follow your interest and inspiration and do the creative task.

Then take the accounting task and move it to the time you had set aside for that high-value creative task.

You can start to see how scheduling tasks creates purpose, and also flexibility in your day.

It's not that you can't rearrange your schedule, it's just that everything needs to stay in your schedule. When you wake up every day you will first reconnect with your values, and then review your schedule and start working on your tasks.

There are going to be times when you look at your day and might say, "Wow, I don't know what to do, I don't know how to do it, or I don't want to do it."

If you don't know what to do, then you might consider more in-depth project planning, or to get a mentor or a coach to help you create a project plan that's more well-defined.

If you don't know how to do it, then decide if you want to

- learn how to do it
- find a way around doing it
- hire somebody to do it for you.

If you don't want to do it, then there's an opportunity to check in again and say, "Is this really a high-value task?" If it is a high-value task and you don't want to do it, then that's what we will talking about in the next chapter.

7. *Measure and assess their progress regularly*

The final step is to evaluate your progress. At the end of every week, I usually do this on Friday afternoon, but different people do it different times, I suggest you block out at least two hours and reconnect with your vision. Step out of working in your business and take the time to work on your business. Here are the steps I suggest:

1. Reconnect with your vision and goals
2. Review your progress
3. Consider opportunity cost

Reconnect with your vision and goals

Reconnect with your vision and your goals, and check to see that the goals you are working on are still the most important. In fast-moving companies, sometimes something that was absolutely urgent last week becomes redundant this week.

It's important to be clear that there's a difference between deciding that a goal is not important anymore and going after the next 'bright shiny object'. You have to be honest with yourself in that. We're going to talk about this in the next chapter.

The question really is: "Am I uncomfortable working toward this goal because it's difficult for me for some reason or I just don't want to do it, but it really would move my business forward, or is it really no longer relevant?"

It's important for you to have self-awareness about what kind of tasks are difficult for you. It might be really difficult for you to reach out to customers, or it might be really difficult for you to learn how to use a new piece of technology, or it might be really difficult for you to do certain tasks. Everybody has different things that are easy or difficult for them, so understanding what is easy or difficult for you will help you to have more clarity around whether this goal is still important.

Review your progress

Check how your projects and sub-projects are doing against the key performance indicators. If analyzing or capturing the data for your key performance indicators is complex, you might not do this every week.

On the other hand, if your KPIs involve how many 'likes' you have on Facebook, how many downloads, or sales, site traffic, profit cost, number of new customers, then go ahead and do it each week. It will give you the satisfaction of being current with all the moving parts of your business, that you are moving towards your goal, and give you some motivation to carry you into the next week.

Checking these indicators can be uplifting and help you feel good about your business and the progress you are making towards your vision.

Opportunity cost

Look at the opportunity cost of doing what you are doing: "Is there something else I could be doing that's more important than this? Is there an emotional cost, is doing this making me miserable?"

Another thing to consider when re-evaluating, and this is something that I've learned working with a lot of venture capital companies, is the concept of pivoting. Many small companies that eventually make it big don't end up looking at all like their original plan five, or ten, or even one year earlier.

Successful entrepreneurs are able to shift, to pivot, and be flexible with their ideas and expand into new areas as the market dictates.

For example, at one point some friends of mine and I started a Java training company, and within six months we were doing high-level strategic consulting. We were still working with Java, but we were doing more consultative work.

At that time, big companies like IBM desperately needed Java training and Java consulting, and we were in a perfect position to do that. Our company was eventually purchased by a venture capital company for two reasons: we were able to pivot and go in a new direction, and because we were flexible in terms of knowing what our values were and what we wanted, but being flexible about how we actually got to that.

The final thing to remember is to have a level of comfort around failure. Learn to look at failure as feedback and a natural part of growth, rather than as a disaster.

For example, I helped a CEO to found an e-commerce business. We built it up, but we made the mistake of fulfilling all our orders through one manufacturer. The sales were great and the money was pouring in, and then one day that manufacturer said, "We're not going to sell to you anymore,". They changed their entire corporate policies to not allow people to sell their products online.

Our business folded less than two months later. If we had diversified our marketing into two different manufacturers, then the company might still be around. It was a difficult and unpleasant time, and it taught me to to diversify. There were times when I felt like a failure, but I took on the feedback and the next time I was working on a business, I was able to help them avoid that mistake.

Summary

All you need is the plan, the roadmap, and the courage to press on to your destination. Earl Nightingale

A little project planning goes a long way when you are an entrepreneur.

Entrepreneurs need to know where they're going and how they are going to get there. If you are a solo entrepreneur this is especially important. Getting all the moving parts out of your head and into a plan and a schedule is going to free your mind up for even more creativity and creative problem solving – one of the things that entrepreneurial types are really good at.

A project plan is your insurance policy against emotional setbacks and slippages in your timelines. Support your creative inclinations by breaking your business down into component parts and get it into a schedule. Get a taste of success with your minimum viable product early on, or gather information that you can build on. Set some measures to tell you when you're being successful. Review often, check in with your vision every day, revise as needed and enjoy the satisfaction of making progress.

In the next chapter I will give you a blueprint for your success as an entrepreneur.

CONCLUSION

The Entrepreneurs Success Blueprint

*"The three great essentials to achieve anything worthwhile are,
first, hard work; second, stick-to-itiveness; third, common sense."*
~ Thomas A. Edison

I'm sitting at one of my favorite restaurants in Bali. I've just finished packing and now I'm tidying up a few loose ends on the computer. Tonight I'm flying business class to Athens to vacation on a Greek island for a week, considering how to conclude this book.

Now I'm back.

I love crowdsourcing, so I asked a number of pre-readers what they would like to see in the conclusion. Here were the answers.

1. The Entrepreneurs Success Blueprint – Summary and Review
2. My story – where am I now
3. Next steps – Putting it into action

The Entrepreneurs Success Blueprint

When we start a new project, we usually have some idea of what we want to accomplish, or the result we want.

What is a 'blueprint'? It's a design plan. It's a plan of how to design something. The Success Blueprint is the blueprint on how to design success.

Depending on the project and on you, these steps may unfold in different orders. This is your personal Entrepreneurs Success Blueprint. There are four ways they can unfold.

1.   You are just getting started and you have an amorphous idea of what you want to accomplish. Maybe you take desultory steps toward accomplishing it, but you don't have a crystal clear idea of your outcome. You probably don't have products or services yet. You are just starting your journey to creating something new. Maybe you've been muddling around a bit and not really having any results, or maybe you are starting fresh.

This is an ideal position to be in as a reader of this book. I would suggest that your first task would be to really understand your values – so work on Chapter 3.

2.   You have a pretty clear picture of what you want, you may have some sales, and you often feel like you spend a lot of time working on stuff that is not the most important stuff. Chances are you're feeling really unproductive and like you are not moving the needle forward.

I would suggest that you reconnect with your values, and then really dig into creating a Success Roadmap. Use this as a step-by-step program to help you determine how to:

- Pare down your list of tasks by either outsourcing or deleting many of them

- Focus on the highest value tasks that will give you the most value for your energy
- Clearly track your success

3. You know what the best things to do every day are, and you are just not doing them. Then, again, I suggest that you reconnect with your values and start to explore what limiting beliefs are impacting your life.

4. You feel like you have great productivity and you have good clients and sales, and you are not really as happy as you really want to be. There are a couple of things that could be going on here:

- You're not working in your area of genius, and you might want to explore systematizing your business so you can focus on the tasks that really light you up.
- You're not aligned with your values. Try the values exercise in Chapter 3.
- You might have some limiting beliefs around happiness and success. Check out the list of limiting beliefs and see which ones resonate for you.

A Note on Limiting Beliefs

Everyone has limiting beliefs. I do, you do, the Dalai Lama does… I think it's the nature of humanity. On the other hand, not everyone lets those beliefs hold them back.

Aligning with possibility and shifting limiting beliefs is one of the reasons why even coaches have coaches. I remember being at a presentation by Brendon Burchard (the New York Times best-selling author of *The Motivation Manifesto, Life's Golden Ticket, The Charge,* and *The Millionaire Messenger*) and him saying that he gets support from five (5!) different coaches.

I have a coach. I also am very aware of my limiting beliefs and work on them in some way or another almost every day. There are days when I wake up afraid, but whereas in the past I would let that impact my day (and my productivity), now I have the tools to notice it (the critical first step) and transform it.

My Story

Throughout this book I've shared stories of my life. They haven't all been pretty, and they haven't been in order. In many ways I've lived a very happy life, and I've also had some really horrible things happen in my life. While I am glad for the person I am now, if I could go back, I would make some changes (I know that's an unpopular viewpoint…).

Where am I now? As of June 2016 I'm still traveling around the world. I'm exploring different co-working spaces, writing, facilitating groups in setting their goals and creating plans, and working with individuals on the Success Zone process.

I've been asked to create a weekend workshop going through the Success Zone and Access Your Power process, and I'm exploring the options.

Action Steps

The purpose of this book is to help you to be more successful. To help you get you into the Success Zone and stay there!

www.ingramcontent.com/pod-product-compliance
Lightning Source LLC
Chambersburg PA
CBHW061153040426
42445CB00013B/1666